Real Snowmen

This is a big snowman.
Have you ever made
a snowman? Have you ever
made a big snowman?

Did you give your snowman eyes?

Did you give your snowman a nose?

Did your snowman look real?

4

DO YOU

?

page 2

page 12

Jeremy Taylor

**Story illustrated by
Steve May**

Before Reading

Find out about

- Strange creatures like huge snowmen, called Yeti

Tricky words

- snowman
- eyes
- real
- people
- Nepal
- huge
- footprints

Introduce these tricky words and help the reader when they come across them later!

Text starter

Some people say there are real snowmen who live in the mountains in Nepal. They call these huge white creatures Yeti.

People say there are
real snowmen.

They say the real snowmen
live in the snow in Nepal.

These snowmen are called Yeti.

People say they have seen Yeti.

They have seen Yeti in the snow in Nepal.

They say the Yeti are huge.

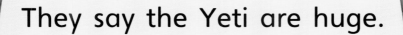

They say the Yeti have white fur.

They say the Yeti are like huge snowmen.

People say they have seen footprints in the snow.

They say the footprints are huge.

They say the Yeti made these footprints.

How big do you think this footprint is?

Did the Yeti make the huge footprints in the snow?

What do you think?

Are there real snowmen called Yeti?
What do you think?

Quiz

Text Detective

- What do people say the Yeti look like?
- Would you like to meet a Yeti?

Word Detective

- **Phonic Focus:** Blending three phonemes
  Page 3: Can you sound out 'big'?
- Page 9: Find a word that means 'very big'.
- Page 9: Find a word made from two words.

Super Speller

Read these words:

think   made   say

Now try to spell them!

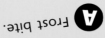

HA! HA! HA!

Q What do you get if you cross a shark with a snowball?

A Frost bite.

In this story

 Tom

Kim

Tricky words

- skateboard
- wheel
- skate
- tried
- another
- snowboard

Introduce these tricky words and help the reader when they come across them later!

Story starter

Tom likes all kinds of sport. One day, he was on his old skateboard when a wheel came off. Kim wanted Tom to stop, but Tom didn't want to stop.

The Old Skateboard

Tom was on his old skateboard.

"Oh no!" cried Tom. "A wheel has come off!"

"You must stop," said Kim. "You can't skate with three wheels!"

But Tom didn't want to stop.
He tried to skate with three
wheels but just then ...

"Oh no!" cried Tom. "Another wheel has come off!"

"You must stop now," said Kim. "You can't skate with two wheels!"

Do you think that Tom can keep going now?

But Tom didn't want to stop. He tried to skate with two wheels. But just then ...

17

"Oh no!" cried Tom. "Another
wheel has come off!"
"You can't skate with one
wheel!" said Kim.

But Tom tried to skate with one wheel ...

"Oh no!" cried Tom. "Another wheel has come off!"
"You can't skate with no wheels!" said Kim.

"Look, Kim!" said Tom.

What do you think will happen now?

"I had an old skateboard ...

but now I have a snowboard!"

Quiz

Text Detective

- What does Tom turn his skateboard into?
- Do you think Tom was clever?

Word Detective

- **Phonic Focus:** Blending three phonemes

  Page 15: Can you sound out 'but'?
- Page 14: Which two words make up the word 'can't'?
- Page 18: Can you find the word 'another'?

Super Speller

Read these words:

stop   want   come

Now try to spell them!

HA! HA! HA!

Q What do cats call mice on skateboards?

A Meals on wheels.